The Chris Letters

From The Source

BALBOA.
PRESS
A DIVISION OF HAY HOUSE

ISBN: 978-1-4525-5872-1 (sc)
ISBN: 978-1-4525-5871-4 (e)

Library of Congress Control Number: 2012917026

Balboa Press books may be ordered through booksellers or by contacting:

Balboa Press
A Division of Hay House
1663 Liberty Drive
Bloomington, IN 47403
www.balboapress.com
1-(877) 407-4847

Printed in the United States of America

Balboa Press rev. date: 09/17/2012

INTRODUCTION

The following work is a series of letters that consists of knowledge that was taken from an ancient source called the Book of Life. You will not find this book in any library on earth. It is from the Spiritual dimension, yet its existence is quite substantive, even though it has no physical form. Much of its content has been conveyed to you through the use of a difficult process of inter-dimensional communication – from the spiritual dimension to that of your physical dimension. There were many involved who were active participants in the sourcing and the providing of this ancient knowledge into simple readable form so that mankind may benefit.

We have provided to you a series of letters that are written in a progressive manner so that all who read and access this knowledge may be able to absorb and digest its content in measured amounts. All who read these pages will be challenged to their very core as there are thousands of years of life on earth that have effectively obscured this knowledge from man's view.

Mankind has a dilemma that must be addressed and laid to rest in order for a healing to take place within each, and for his world. The following letters are written so that each one of you may address the age old questions of who we really are and what our purpose here on earth truly is. It is all so much simpler than we have thought it to be, however, no less challenging. The mind has been trained over many lifetimes in ways that have led each further and further a field from our own true nature. Yet, there are ways to find ones true self once again, even in the midst of a seemingly chaotic world.

Love, joy, happiness and prosperity can all be sourced from the knowledge conveyed in these letters to mankind. It is just in the knowing and then in the doing. All the tools needed are contained in the following manuscripts that will serve as an illuminating guidepost for each, as they once again make their way into the light of joy and enlightenment where we are all meant to reside.

Chris letter 8

In the softness of night, or perhaps in the crispness of the morning early on – when the heavy thrust of man's world begins to ebb, or has not yet started its engines. Perhaps as little ones, we may take a quiet moment to peer deep within ourselves and ask what it is that we truly want.

Is it just things of the Earth? Is it recognition from our fellow man, or is it a special favor from one who holds our passion? Are not all these things transient and temporary? As we acquire them all in our own accordance, does not their luster dim? Why is this? Why, if the Earth contains not that of satisfaction to me, then what else may I look to?

The answer lies deep within little one, for, indeed, the Earth should lose its brilliance. For all of its measure that you acquire is represented only by the feeling that is generated within you. Yet, that which sustains you is the universal energy and force of Supreme Love. It courses through all in the sustaining of all life. It is not a split second passion or grinding emotion to acquire and accumulate. One's Soul need not rush to accumulate from another that which it already has to give. All the love you have to give is not temporary, nor is it dependent on any social restriction. All the love you have to give shall not lower your own fill and measure within as you so dole it out. For, remember the Law of Cause and Effect. It says: "as you so give, so you shall receive". It matters not whether another is deserved in the eyes of society. The law takes care of them as well as you.

Thus, you may give freely in your own measure of love – to ALL those you pass, and to all those with whom you deal. For even if they are not outwardly responsive and understanding, it matters not; their Soul knows and the Law knows and most importantly and crucially, YOU KNOW.

Yours, Chris

©

Indeed little one, a Soul need not purchase its own love in the stalls of man's social market. That which is inherently you, cannot be lost to any sad occasion, nor may another's be kept and saved in a bottle. No need; and there is no need for the mixing of hostility and anger in the blame of love. For one is an emotion born of the physical influence, and the latter equals the constant pulse of the very core of your being.

No need, little one to blame ones own pain and sorrow on another, for at one time or another their suffering shall be your equal. Truly, there is no useful solace in the pain of another for ANY reason of man. The quality of revenge and spite shall only serve as a breeding ground for same.

Why is this? It is because it is the Law. All things, all life of earth, and all life not of earth must and do adhere to the Law of Cause and Effect.

Though you may see your world as imbalanced, it is only to the extent of your own world and not that of others. Why does man continue to add to his own world of imbalance? It is because his insight is clouded by what he sees, hears, smells, touches, and tastes. It is these five senses that place him into a de-orientation away from his own vibrational sense of on going, operational love force.

In the five sense realm of the physical, man has observed for eons of time the way of the animal and its potentials. In so doing he has misconstrued Cause and Effect to operate only in the immediate and near term; but such is actually not the case. Because of the mechanics of the energy you cannot see, man, in choice, triggers deep down line effects in his causative choices. Thus, the old saying: That, which goes around, comes around; and vastly more-so than man in his earth born society could ever imagine.

Any thought or act of love shall be returned to you in appropriate form and time. Any thought or act of hate, anger or violence shall also return to you in its full measure.

Since the Law itself and the order of carrying out the Law is based and processed in the unseen non-physical dimension, you give it little credence. Man goes willy nilly in his attempt to produce peace, justice and restitution out of anger and self justified value judgments. The Law cares not if you are Christian, Judean, Islamic, American, Russian, etc; if you do anything at all in hate or self righteous anger, no matter how justified you are in the eyes of self and society, then like thought and action shall find its way back to you fully. THIS is why history constantly repeats itself. THIS is why lessons are not learned.

Make no mistake; the lesson does NOT end with the passing of your biology into the ground. The Soul remains intact in Limbo with its lesson attached to it until another return is made. This is the way of it for all. Indeed ALL – King, Queen, Baker, Butcher, Priest. It matters not your earthly societal position. For ALL such positions are appointments by man, and NOT the One Soul.

So, you see, all of mankind already has his ultimate judicial system. It is recorded within and there is no shading of the facts with self. For within, there lies the mechanism to change wrong to right. How? Only in love, kindness, compassion and forgiveness may resolution be made.

When all such resolution is made, then you shall not return again to the trapped state you now know. You shall indeed be free in the ultimate sense of the word.

Yours, Chris

©

Chris Letter 10

Indeed, what IS a Soul? Ah, the age old question. Is it something that exists only for consideration on a particular day designated by man as "holy"? Is it something to be considered only in the birthing of physical life and then in the termination of physical life? What then for goodness sakes?

Man addresses it in many a way. In one vein, he takes it upon himself to actually dictate to another their measure of Soul worth. In another, he would even go so far as to render judgment in determining the outcome of another's Soul in this world, and the next.

Mark well oh purveyors of doom and gloom, the only outcome of another you may determine in life or death is that of their physical body. For their Soul is as yours – inviolate, and absolutely and totally indestructible. No one on earth has spiritual license for condemnation of another that shall render them lifeless or invalidated as a Soul. If one attempts such, they only impede their own progress along the path towards re-perfection in all love, harmony, kindness and compassion towards self and his fellow man.

So, again, what actually is a Soul? A Soul is a non physical being, a person – the inner person that you cannot see with your own physical mental faculties or with any sort of physical device. All the same, it is the defining core of your being – that, which gives you life, even in the physical dimension, for through the Soul, comes the elemental life force of the Universe that sustains your being through birth and death of your biology. This elemental, source energy is at the core of ALL life. It has to come from somewhere, and the unseen, higher dimension is the generator of universal life everywhere – in all worlds including and even beyond your own. The Soul of mankind is the highest form of existence in the Universe, as it contains all the properties of the great One Soul from which it came. Do not mistake the regression of man in his earthly expressions of fear and hate as equating with the high principles and expressions of a pure Soul. Man, in his physical form, has fallen from grace through his mind, ego and intellect due to his exposure to the survival engines of the physical beings that he occupies in life after life. Yet, the Soul is not invaded. It simply retreats in non interference and non resistance – although still remaining as your source of life.

Take note: You always know yourself to be, as life progresses on and on through timeless passages and cycles of your spiritual and physical existence. The "you" that you know yourself to be in all moments of time never ceases. Events come and go. Lifetimes come and go. You regress and you advance until one day you shed the earthly existence altogether – returning to your original pure state of an unfettered Soul, but with all the events, lifetimes and experiences recorded within. You cannot escape your self – that which you truly are within, that is the "you" that lives on through eons of time, whether surrounded by physical existence, or as spirit alone, remains indestructible, and cannot be terminated by any force known to man OR spirit.

There are the Soul Laws of Choice, Communication, Faith, Cancellation and Love that comprise the "you" that are not of your world or body. There are vast ramifications and powers behind these Laws and are little understood by man on earth, yet render each greatly expanded abilities and potentials that are taken for granted in your world. In your higher states, you are gifted with the ability to travel whole Universes when not in your present trapped conditions. Such a thing is possible not by magic or miracle, but by the operation and function of laws that are quite alien to the limitations of the physical world. This is why they are not recognized – simply because you as a Soul have at one far time ago, chosen to enter a totally foreign environment; and in so doing you have lost knowledge and abilities of self that remain in waiting to be set free.

It is now time to apprise man of that which governs his many functions and actions. In so doing all of the confusions shall be brought to task.

Yours, Chris

©

Why does one fear? Indeed it is for ones own person in all cases. For even if a loved one should depart our presence, is it not our own concern for self that we are left with after they have taken our leave. How can one possibly "feel" for another? They cannot. One may only "feel" for themselves in REGARDS to another.

We need not fear at all, for to fear is by teaching of man in his world. We are not OF that world. We are all infinite beings and we shall remain so. Is such not the very definition of infinity itself – to remain always…

You see, we fear because we have taught ourselves to do so by observing the first potential of fear within the body and the animal. Such a potential is necessary for its survival, because they are not eternal beings in their given form at birth. They must drive to the instincts of immediate survival and procreation in order to sustain their species. Though Homo Sapiens is a species of the Earth, you are not. You are an infinite being temporarily trapped in the physical form.

Because man has choice, he has the ability to take the simple instinct of the animals fear and then intellectually expand upon it into concepts of war, hate, anger, frustration and condemnation. So as the animal, he hurls these concepts at one another in hopes of alleviating them. However, the animal only reacts to the moment. It does not expand its responses into revenge and contrived confrontations of whole populations. Indeed not. It cannot. It only reacts to the moment. Therefore Cause and Effect is limited in its down line results – balance is maintained.

Choice is an impartial Law; it allows for man to expand upon fear to suit his own immediate needs of earthly satisfaction; however, the Law of Cause and Effect does not allow man to escape the down line results.

Indeed, so as you expand in fear so shall you reap in fear on a later date. That date is not known, for the Law has no regard for the clock. It is the same with love. The Law will bear fruit as well. It must, for the Law is of the Universe, and not of man.

Yours, Chris

©

Chris letter 12

Perhaps, little one, you are now beginning to question the standard fare of worldly consumption to the mind. Perhaps you even ask: But what of the Bible? Does it not teach fear in that my very soul is in jeopardy? Indeed it does, and those passages therein that purvey such were placed into the original manuscripts of selection by the Church of Man. Indeed, there are those who know this, and upon their reading of this message, they shall fear for their very worldly position. For their position depends upon their holding the fear of man captive by these ancient alterations of that which was originally given to man by Christ. Only certain manuscripts of many were chosen to be entered into what is now known as the Bible. Then in the fourth century, the Church of Man altered these to inject raw fear into the mainstream of society.

The original manuscripts of Christ's teachings are presently held by this Church of Man and in due course these teachings shall surface to reveal the infinite quality of all Souls.

Indeed, who shall benefit from this revealing? All, yes ALL – even, and most of all, those who so finally choose to expose the ancient hoax of man. For these Souls who now occupy such seats of power are the one and the same who once chose and acted to remove the eternal teachings of Christ from public view. This statement shall ring out as a bell of antiquity to those who are of present. Indeed, all Souls are old Souls in that all here on this plane of Earth in the now have been here before – many times before.

Yours, Chris

©

Indeed, who would so dare to question the Bible itself? It is man who has questioned it as it is man who originally sequestered, and then altered the manuscripts.

Even so, there was not a bolt of lightening that came forth from the sky in a manner of angry rebuke from the heavens.

Indeed, man supplies his own bolt of lightening in all cases of transgression. Consider: If the fear concept had not been injected into the manuscripts that were chosen, then perhaps all of mankind would have taken a different course. The Law of Cause and Effect does not cease its motion with time. So as fear has been bartered and sold upon the open market of mans choices for better than 2000 Earth years, so it is now manifesting in society and populations everywhere.

If it were allowed to be known that fear and the way of the animal would not produce love and peace as its effect, would not those concerned think twice before launching crusades against his fellow man? Were it allowed to be known early on that for each decision and choice made by each individual in the fear base of the animal – it would attach itself to that individual in Karma, thus requiring each to return to Earth in the resolving of it? Were it known that all extended acts and choices made in fear and anger, no matter what the earthly justification, would require restitution and that the greatest harm is not to the other, but SELF. Would you not think twice as a thinking individual before harming YOURSELF in such a way?

THIS is why it is best to turn away from the urge to seek revenge. Indeed, it is not out of weakness and shrinking, spineless fear that one is best advised to forgive. It is because as you so react in anger and fear, so shall a like reaction make its way to you bye and bye; and then in addition to finally resolving the incident of hurt and harm, one must have their own hurt and harm accepted and released in love, forgiveness and compassion for self and others. This accepting and releasing of self and others from the bond of hate and fear is called Cancellation. It is an actual Law of the Soul and as such it allows us to undo all the harm done in past and present. Well it is for man that such a Law exists.

Yours, Chris

©

Chris Letter 14

Perhaps now, little one, the order of man is beginning to peek through as a ray of light emits between the darkness of storm.

Indeed, it is not mans' regression and transgressions that mark his true heritage, but the knowledge that each little one on earth this day does indeed possess a Soul, and that such is the best news yet to come in 2000 years of man's time.

Why so? Because each possesses an infinite capacity to love self and others; and it is indeed alright for us to do so. For each time we do, and like, IMMEDIATE results do not follow, know and understand that the Law of Cause and Effect does not always unfold on man's perceived and presumed schedule. Still, you may have no doubt, the affect WILL manifest in its own proper order and time. Perhaps such delay is a part of the resolving and undoing of that which we have previously perpetrated upon others; and to make restitution, some further cancellation of Karma through additional measures of love and forgiveness must be attended to. Know full well that the day of full accounting will surely surface in due time and order. There is no side stepping the law for it is sure, impartial and constant in its affects, as is gravity upon a stone dropped from a cliff. You see, gravity is applied through physical law with its affects instantly visible and manifest. Whereas, Karma is a law of the non physical - given to its processing in non-time; unseen, but just as sure in its outcome Ah, but therein lies the good news, as no good deed or thought goes unrecorded; nor is it ever lost. From an understanding of the Law, faith may turn to knowing. Where there is knowing, doubt is dismissed and resolve holds fast and steady providing safe passage through rough Karmic seas.

So, fear not little one, it is alright to give, for only in such a manner shall we know true satisfaction and peace within. Things of the earth belong to the earth in that they always return to the earth.

That of the Soul shall return to you and remain with you, for it is of you and part of you throughout the infinite circle of life.

Each shall not resolve their transgressions in a single day for it was greater than one day in the making. Yet, forgiveness and cancellation allows for a speedier return than the falling. Such are the means of the Law in its orderly workings.

Yours, Chris

©

Funny, how we have such little sense of the temporary nature of our stay in this world. Why is this? It is because while our physical ends on some particular day, we as thinking, living beings do not – in that we always have only a sense of the now that is never ending. Indeed, we may CONSIDER both the past and the future, but we cannot live it until it actually becomes part of the now; and in that manner you shall never live in the past nor shall you ever live in the future. Only in the now do you exist and shall you always exist. Such a fact does not mean that events stand still. No indeed, they do not, but time does. The Soul does not know of this thing man calls time. It does not care of it for it knows it cannot re-live the past nor can it live the future while in the now.

Mumbo jumbo, not at all, for what is done, is done and that which is to come will come.

We cannot change the past with fear and regret of it. We may cancel it though, by emitting love and understanding in the present. We cannot make the future happen before its time; but we can shape its events by emitting love and understanding to selves and all those around us. For you see time is a function of Cause and Effect. Time does not really exist – only do events and experience EXIST – not to you in the past nor in the future, but only really in the NOW. Such is where the ongoing sum of your reality lies.

So, if we do not allow the days love and compassion to surface, then we have missed an opportunity, for that day shall not return to you. Opportunity shall render itself unto you by the flow of events, not by time. Time is only a concept in mans mind. It is events that are real, and well it is that we take them immediately in hand, for each life cycle upon earth is limited in events by the duration of your physical, and that each life cycle is for the sole and express purpose of returning to the Souls own nature – that of love, kindness, compassion and allowance for all men and all things. Indeed, THIS is mans purpose on earth.

Yours, Chris

©

Chris Letter 16

The hard nut of life in this world is not one to be cracked, but is to be seen for what it is. There is much running of to and fro in your world. There is a frantic quality to many as they rush to the events of the day. All are groping and grasping outward for some sign of deeper meaning to their own individual lives.

Some attempt to find it in politics, some in the stalls of the money changers. Others attempt to find love and harmony in their passions towards others; thus looking to another and others of the world for self-sustainment.

You see, all the creatures of the earth are of limited design capability in that they MUST seek outwardly for sustenance in survival and procreation lest their species die out. Even if their species should die, it is no tragedy to them, for they do not think in terms of tragedy. However, since mans intellect is a function of the Souls' Law of Choice and Communication, he has created his mind which acts as a bridge between the physical and the Soul, which is not OF the physical. Because the mind is impartial in its ability to apply direction of choice, and the Soul does not interfere with a heavy hand; we have constructed huge constructs of fear based upon the survival laws and potentials of our physical. Our physical is no less an animal than the monkey in the zoo. Blasphemy? Indeed not, for each of us has a Soul contained therein and though each Soul on earth may be trapped for a time, it is still OF itself - totally intact in its pure elemental state, it stands in waiting for the mind to finally respond by choosing a path of non resistance and non interference with self and others. For, until we choose as such, the heavy inducements of the animal shall bear weight upon our choices, and we shall remain in our present state – not knowing why – but remaining just the same.

If you listen, respond to, and project the gentle urgings of the Soul in love, forgiveness, harmony, non resistance and non interference towards self and others, you shall indeed be rewarded in like manner in return. You shall not be left to the harshness of the world. Remember the Law of Cause and Effect. It is immutable as the Law of gravity, and shall bear the fruits of your choices; there can be no other result. You need only understand that it works in its own time, which is non-time; which is to say that the Law's seeking, finding and processing of the perfect effect, is done out of your view. You cannot see its workings in the dimension from which it comes, so you travail, and give up when it does not produce on your time line, and in the fashion which you have created in your mind. The event produced may be a surprise to you, and come, seemingly, from out of nowhere; but that is the way of the Law.

Indeed, all is of a process in the return to your original state of grace; but was it not a process in your falling?

Yours, Chris

©

Who is it that says: "Repent you Sinners" Is it God? Is it Christ himself? Indeed not. No, it is the word of man who points the finger of judgment at others.

The Soul of each is in need of no middle man to point out the transgressions of self. Indeed, it is the Soul itself that is charged with its OWN process of judgment and restitution. Each Soul knows very well the deeds of self, and it does so respond to present ones self with gainful opportunity to resolve all such Karmic deeds.

He who points the finger of judgment to another must be prepared to make accounting to their OWN self for such acts.

No man is God to others. None are Souls over other Souls. A Soul knows itself and that is sufficient. Why? Because it is designed as a fully operational self contained unit of ones own responsibility. How can this be and still have universal balance? Must there not be leaders, intercessionists, policemen of the Soul?

Not so, each Soul has the capacity to choose in universal love and balance; as you so choose in love, all else is seen to. Such is the genius in its simplicity. The Law of Cause and Effect shall invoke itself at every turn.

Look not to the harsh judgment of man who would render a final appraisal of your human and spiritual progress, but to your own Soul within, for therein lies the where-with-all to do so - the source of ALL answers to all things needed for each Soul to make good their journey in return to the One Soul.

Yours, Chris

©

Chris Letter 18

Perhaps the greatest transgression to man done in the 4th Century Revision Council, were those deletions and revisions that took away the knowledge of man as an eternal being. In one stroke of the quill, at each mention of the Souls infinite quality, the light was blotted out for centuries. From that point on, man would be bound to the Church of Man by the yoke of fear in the concept of death to your Soul, lest you fall into file and repent self to the middle man.

For century upon century man has been instructed by man, not God or Christ, that if he does not profess self to a doctrine of man, then he shall burn!! Burn indeed... Before the manuscripts were changed, and the epistles revised, they taught not the doom of billions, but the eternal life of all Souls – no matter how entrenched in the Karma of fear.

Burn indeed; none shall burn, NONE. All are Souls and all, yes all one day shall know the total love of their own Soul – even those who perpetrated two thousand years of hoax upon their brothers. For it is each Soul's charge that you shall return to earth again and again until sufficient unto the day when love of self, and love of others fully exceeds that measure of karmic regression accumulated in all of your journeys through each earth life cycle. Indeed, this is the Karmic circle of restitution that all must undergo. Even those rich in spirit, must conduct a full accounting of self, as must all others. In this we are all equal and of the same brotherhood. One is well advised to extend a helping hand to your fellow Soul traveler, which is a great sum different than the pointing of the finger of judgment to your brothers of earth.

Yours, Chris

©

Who is Satan??? Is he male, female, black, white, yellow or red skinned? If not that, is he as a ghost that flits around on Halloween night frightening innocent people from their wits; or is he a former person with spiritual license to invade other Souls at will, thus wreaking universal havoc?

He is NONE of these things – NONE. When man is begotten by ill events he tends to blame it on one or a combination of three things: Satan, an angry God or somebody else. Why do we not think to blame our own ills upon our own selves? Indeed we should, for this is the way of it all. There is not one single thing of an ill nature that happens to you that is not of the Law that YOU invoke along the way.

When something happens seemingly out of the blue, it appears to be from unseen forces. It is, but those forces are merely the down line out workings of the Cosmic and Soul Laws that YOU have set into motion. Not an angry God, Satan OR your fellow Souls.

If you perpetrate regressive behavior upon another, then it shall return to you somewhere in time. Indeed, all, yes all of mans negative surprises are due to Natural Law, and the laws you are empowered with as Souls that you invoke along the way. If this is so, does it not follow that the answer to all of the world's woes lies in the power of each to choose in love rather than anger? Indeed it does follow, and yes it is that SIMPLE. For if this is how the Law is, and it IS, then it indeed is that simple.

All of the fighting, blaming, suing, hating and judging will not invoke the Law of Cause and Effect to produce LOVE. It is just that simple and logical.

Do not think that one act of love on your part will cancel all the transgressions of world and self. NO ONE is saved in a moment or a day. To reverse the great wheel already in motion, will take a long concerted effort; but it is the ONLY way out for ALL.

No man of letters or of charismatic oration can bestow salvation upon you, thus instantly cancelling all of your past misdeeds to others. He cannot even do such for himself, let alone another Soul. All Souls are independent in that they must account for their own misdeeds – even those who CLAIM to represent other Souls. ALL must face the Law – it is impartial.

Yours, Chris

©

Chris Letter 20

Then who, indeed, is Christ? Is he person, spirit, God? The man Jesus was a person in the re-perfected state of the Christ Spirit. The man Jesus is a Soul as you are a Soul. He appoints himself no special position OVER you. All Souls are equal in their status and elemental makeup. Jesus was a teacher of man, a deliverer of good news. His mission was to lift the veil of ignorance and shine the light of love and knowledge upon mankind, for he had clear sight and vision of both worlds – a rare thing amongst men. He made his way about teaching and demonstrating the power of love that springs from the Soul, as he was well aware that your own rate of choice in the Supreme Law of Love determines your relative position in the Christ Spirit.

What IS love from the perspective of the Soul, and what did the man Jesus say of it? It is the greatest power in the Universe from which springs all of creation in its infinite capacity. Conversely, would you think creation springs from some lifeless neutral zone, or perhaps a dark void where a random spark initiates life out of chaos? Such is not the way of it. Love from the physical world is not the same as Love from the Soul. Love from the Soul in its highest state can create and sustain life. Does it conform and come from natural law? Indeed it does; and from the Soul's perspective it is the greatest power in the Universe. So why does not God, or the Soul within man in his human clothing, exert the force and power of Love from the Soul and make everything right and good. It cannot, as the Soul also abides by certain principles of non resistance and non interference. Souls do not interfere with the natural order of things in nature. But the power of love from the Soul is indeed immense, and as each progresses out of the darkness of the veil cast from the physical, they begin to experience this power. So as room is made within from the expansion of consciousness, the Soul will act to fill the void with this loving power.

In the biology of the physical there is also love, but of a different nature. It is the great balancer that tempers nature's survival engines, that sustains harmony and temperance in the beast, as well as all other creatures. However, it is of a different order than that of the Soul. The Soul in its natural state need not contend with the driving forces of survival. It does not occupy itself with gathering food and water for its sustenance, for its sustenance comes from the elemental loving force of the One Soul - who many choose to call God. This force is eternal, so there is no fear of it ending. It is infinite in supply, so there is no driving necessity from within to protect one's measure of it. There is an awareness and knowing from within the Soul that all is eternally well and cared for in perfect order. Ah yes, there is order to everything in life, though it may not seem so. Mankind, in his human clothing, shall come to know the immense power of this radiant force, but in measures that he can accommodate. He will come to know that this power is vastly more moving than that of any sort of anger or emotion of vengefulness that may spring from the human condition.

Jesus the man did not return to earth in order to assume any worldly position of authority whatsoever. He came to show that all men have Souls and that all men may re-perfect in the Christ Spirit. It was not the intention of the man Jesus that whole populations kill each other off in his name. The man Jesus came to demonstrate that each has a Soul, and that it is not Pagan ritual or any doctrine invented by man that the Soul of each depends upon for their existence. It is God's Laws of Life in nature that guarantees you eternal life.

He came to demonstrate the possibilities of all men of any faith. You see, the Supreme Law of Love, kindness, compassion and forgiveness may be spoken in any language, in any country and by any man, women or child. This is the essence of Christ. Not hate, war, judgment or ritual perpetrated in the NAME of Christ. Indeed, Jesus had many false accusers that would not accept his words OR his deeds at face value. These accusers feared for their worldly positions in the holding of power over their fellow man. The truth, when heard, resonates in the Soul and in the mind of the many thereby threatening to dissolve the false power held by a few.

His mission was to show that even the false accusers may one day know the Christ state of consciousness, as they eventually make gain along their own karmic pathway of restitution.

Yours, Chris

©

Chris Letter 21

If the man Jesus, known as the Christ of ancient times, were to return to your land today, what would he think, feel and do?

Would he be befuddled by mans advance in technology over the centuries? Would he feel lost amongst all of the modern preachers of the day? Would he feel ancient and out of date, touch and place with the times? Indeed he would not. He would NOT marvel at mans technological advancements and say: "Ah, little ones you have come so far! Why look at all the fine cars, trucks, planes, houses, buildings, guns, tanks, battleships and missiles!" No, indeed such would not impress him, for in ancient times, he was able to perform feats that were possible only by the power of a Soul that had access to the workings of higher Universal Law. He possessed and demonstrated the power of love, healing and life itself. He was a teacher and purveyor of knowledge so powerful that it changed the course of mankind for thousands of years to come.

Indeed, you may rest assured he did those things – by the modern technology of the day? No, by having advanced natural abilities that reside in the higher, spiritual dimension available to a perfected Soul: A Soul potential that all men have and that all men may know and experience in their own time and rhythm of life

He would say: "The potential and capability of the Soul may surpass the wonder of any modern feat of man's technology". You see, man's technology in the physical is OF the physical and is therefore sorely limited from a higher dimensional order of advanced expressions. You do not know this because in the pursuit of the survival, procreation and protection potentials of the body, you have lost knowledge and ability to see your own possibilities of a higher and more powerful nature.

"This is why I came in the first place, to inform all that they are OF the Soul and spiritual realm and NOT OF the Animal in its limited, physical realm".

Yours, Chris

©

You think that since man has devised technological ways and means to express the animal instinct, his actions are of any higher order? Indeed they are not; they can be of a lower order than the animal itself. For the animal does not sit in thought to devise ways of rendering his entire species extinct. Man does this in the name of peace.

He thinks that because he drapes himself in a fine suit of clothes and speaks with an artful and educated tongue, that the intellect of it justifies all things – that love is not practical and shall not work in such high places.

Better he stand naked before all, and scrap his intellect along with all his contrived and manufactured expressions of the animals survival instinct.

Such shall work fine for the animal, as it reacts only to the moment. Thus balance is maintained. Not man; because he has choice and a misconception of the Laws of Soul in the workings of Cause and Effect. He bares his teeth in more ways than any animal would begin to consider.

You say, "Pity the poor animal. If the animal could think and talk as man, he would say: Pity the poor man; he runs to and fro using our Laws of Survival and Procreation in ways and means never meant to be devised. Why, what species would ever set itself upon earth and contrive to exterminate its whole population with things called weapons. Indeed, what species!!"

Yours, Chris

©

Chris Letter 23

If the man Jesus returned from ancient times and looked about and around, would he go forth to the most powerful church in the land – to its seat of power and proclaim himself King in return?

Indeed he would not, for such centers of worldly power serve not the Soul of man, but the worldly pursuits of man. The Soul of man does not intend for him to be King of Earth. He need only love self and others about him in totality. To do such a simple task, does he need robes of finery and great halls with spires built upon them in order to express the simple act of love? Indeed not.

If Jesus came and all those about him knew it was he, would he ask each Soul to pay him money for his love and his favor? Indeed not. For, you see he would give of his love freely. Such is the Souls definition of giving: Freely – asking for nothing in return. Only then may such love and gift be returned to you. This is how the Law works.

The Law knows that if you give only to receive gain and harm is perpetrated upon another in the process, then the process shall be the same for you.

Would he declare and found a great Church and name it after himself? No he would not. For, the Soul has its church within. Now, we all adhere to the Law of Originality, and thus each has his own rhythm and path of return to perfection.

The Soul can know comfort in the most barren of ground. Should it need great halls and great leaders to know itself along its own path? Indeed not. It contains all the ingredients for such within self.

Yours, Chris

©

Indeed, why does mankind wander the earth in confusion over the meaning of love? To the animal of earth it is expressed in its drive to procreate and in its drive to protect its mate and offspring, and in its moments of playful respite from acts of survival. This is not a bad thing for the animal, as it allows it to sustain life and balance.

Such is not of the Soul however. Perhaps you feel we tread upon the sacred cow of man in his concept of procreation and family?

Before man came to earth, in Soul form, he did not procreate; he did not have children. His love was not divided into parcels and categories that are representative of the laws of the physical. Indeed not, the love of the Soul imparts a steady pulse of vibrational love in allowance and acceptance for all men and all creatures.

You see a Soul need not have territorial lines drawn to protect its self. The animal does this by design because it is of its own different Laws of Survival and Procreation. However, man, (unlike the animal who acts on instinct alone), through his power of choice, can reverse love into the emotion of hate. Why is this? It is because when he feels threatened, he taps the survival engines of his biology that are constantly running at some level, thus turning his love to anger and hate. It is a survival reaction that rides rough shod over the Soul. The Soul retreats and so he feels justified in his anger over his threatened territory

Man has taken these laws of the species and applied them in greater concept to self by his ability to choose on an ever expanding intellectual basis. In so doing he has adhered to the physical laws of survival throughout his intellectual expansion. He fiercely guards his territory with all means at his disposal. He calls this necessary, lest he should forfeit his worldly gain and lose ground to those who he considers of less Soul value. How wrong he is.

It is his very act of drawing the lines about his physical territories that prevents him from allowing the Soul straight forth into his daily expression. He feels that his love is reserved for his religion, his mate, his children and his country. His Soul balks at these territorial lines drawn. The Soul would bring down all territorial lines and acknowledge the sanctity of all Souls; and in so doing would emit the steady quiet pulse of its love vibration to all. Only in this manner shall man begin to undo that which he has perpetrated upon himself and his poor world for thousands of years.

Yours, Chris

©

Chris Letter 25

If the man of ancient times known as Jesus Christ were to come forth this day, would he declare himself a Christian: Indeed he would not. He would declare himself a Soul; that which all men are.

Would he found a Church based on a doctrine of fear, and point to others of unlike doctrine and say unto them: "You shall all burn in a fiery pit lest you confess and subjugate yourselves beneath me." Indeed he would not. He would declare that all men are valid, equal and intact Souls in the now and forever and ever. No man needs fear for his eternal, spiritual life lest he not declare himself a member of a particular order or church as so created by man.

The order of all men is their Soul. The Soul of man cares not for exclusive rights over another. If you feel that because of your attendance to an organization of man that your Soul cares for such, then you are in for the biggest surprise of all. Man says that God built his church. However, God does not need man to act as his representative in the disposition of other men, nor does man need a keeper for his own Soul. The church of man did not spring forth directly from Mother Nature, however man's Soul most assuredly did, and does not need an agent, nor manager to validate his existence in this life or the next. Does this mean that there is not good and proper wisdom housed in the church of man? Assuredly there is, but that which is of a binding and political nature to man's spirit, is anathema to God and the Soul of man.

For, it is so that all other men of differing doctrine and religious persuasion have the same capacity as you to emit love, kindness, compassion and allowance for self and others. All of these things are qualities of the Soul that resides in each of us. No membership or exclusive rights of any kind are needed to emit these qualities from self. It is that ALL men have Souls that they are even able to dispute ones Soul over another.

For you see it is each man's Soul that has given him a mind to develop the power of intellect, and free will in the choosing of one doctrine or another. The Soul does this because it wishes not to enter into the harsh fray of mans choices made within the survival potentials of the physical animal.

While it remains out of the fray, it supplies each with the constant pulse of loving alternative to choose; and oh yes, it also supplies you with the ability to maintain life in its infinitely sustaining pulse– that which you take for granted.

Yours, Chris

©

Chris Letter 26

Have you perhaps lost a loved one? Does the world not show you favor? Though we strive and strain for happiness, are we somehow left for want?

You see, the world is a proving ground for the past life mistakes of all little ones who are present on earth now. Indeed All. None are here simply to placidly enjoy the fruits of the land. In each tragedy that befalls you and in each loss that you suffer, you may know 100% certain that there is a reckoning in the experience.

If you view those of lofty station and feel envy; do not. For within those of high earthly station, there is an inner burden that may very likely exceed your own. Perhaps their Karma is so great that in a life previous, great sorrow to many was perpetrated. It is now theirs, and our own lot to conduct a reckoning of our past misdeeds.

It is in this light that all tragedy that befalls us should be viewed - as an opportunity more than as a personal calamity. For it is your Soul that has exercised procedure within, that you may be given the opportunity to now cancel past misdeeds. In that all Souls are about the same business at hand, we are free then to understand that all are on the same march homeward.

Though life in the fray of man's world may seem deep and hurtful at times, such hurt itself is indeed the opportunity. For herein lies the very crux of opportunity to bless and release that hurt. It is an inner thing, a thing of vibration that surely binds you to the earth and its constant fray. It MUST be acknowledged as an opportunity to settle accounts with self. It is inner to YOU. Not the fault of another. The gain is yours in the letting go of it.

Nothing, absolutely nothing happens to you by accident, nor without purpose.

Yours, Chris

©

Chris Letter 27

Why is it that we must allow fully for others? Why must we not stop them in their tracks, so that they shall see the light as we do?

Why indeed. There is high purpose in the allowance for ALL things that another may perpetrate. If you should take active your own role in the attempt to block another, then by the Soul's definition you are resisting and interfering. However, you do so because it is the usual and familiar thing to do – the way of the world. The survival and fear potentials of the animal have taught our minds to resist and interfere. Yet, the Soul is of other, higher laws of operation and existence and loathes to operate as such. For each time you resist and interfere with another, no matter WHAT your cause, you cause your very own Soul to retreat further from self in the fray. It is a simple matter of procedure and operation to the Soul. It will not open up to any resistance or interference no matter what the cause to self.

You resist and interfere to preserve your position of world. The Soul does not seek a worldly position, as it has no need to preserve its territory. It has no physical requirements at all. It seeks to come away from such. Consequently, it need seek no bases of worldly power over others in the interest of controlling resources for itself.

The Soul will retreat until you decide and choose in non resistance and non interference. Why? Because the Soul is an infinitely sustainable being – eternally alive -it is tapped directly into the universal life energy source, and does not cycle through stages of birth, growth, waning and finally – death. Such is a simple matter of Universal Laws of Nature and the workings of the dimension of Soul versus the lower sub system dimension of the physical. It is not a matter of doctrine or value judgment of one over another.

Yours, Chris

©

Is it not odd that man is able to apply science to understanding the biological operations of his physical body, yet he has practically no understanding of the higher, natural order BEHIND his biology. Why is this?

It is because nature's orderly balance of the animal's life cycles on earth within the Law of Survival and Procreation, and the first potential of fear, have been expanded by mankind through his intellect into horrific aberrations. Each potential of the physical body: Fear, Hunger, Protection, Satisfaction, Desire, Ecstasy, and Love is an actual instinct built into the physical nervous system that works harmoniously in balance for the animal in nature's wild. However, this natural biological system originally intended solely for the animal, has resulted in thousands of years of induced, deeply entrenched Karmic out-workings for mankind. He does not realize what he is doing to himself, as he takes what is naturally intended only for the animal's survival, and expands upon it with his intellect into concepts of war and revenge. Animals do not seek revenge against one another. They react only to the moment's survival needs.

Man has no clue that so many of his earthly rituals, concepts and dogma built into his order of life have been intellectualized and created through the body's survival engines that are constantly running and influencing the mind as to man's choices. Man's intellect has been perversely shaped over thousands of years from constant exposure as a co-host to the animals fear potentials. Man resides within the animal, and is therefore subject to its influences. He has become so blinded from living within the fear potentials of the animal for so long, that he even applies the same fear based principles to the judging of his own Soul.

A Soul operates by strict laws of functional existence just as your body does – only on a much higher order. Its laws of existence are every bit as definable, though different, from that of your physical. The Soul is not fettered by the physical time, space continuum that your body is tied to in its day to day life. The Soul remains intact within the non time, non linear continuum that is of a higher dimension. Souls do not die from age, disease, or lack of sustenance. Only physical bodies cease operation and fade to dust. However, once physical death occurs, the Soul is set free and continues to live on eternally with your personality intact.

It is absolute superstition to think that a Soul builds its laws of operation and existence around varying doctrines and concepts that are largely born out of the fear base of the animal survival system. Does it seem reasonable that universal, operational order would have your Soul burning in hell simply because you fail to do what some one else tells you to do? No man, nor organization of man, has that kind of power over the natural order of the Universe. There are Laws of existence that are immutable and inviolate, and set eternally into stone. Natural Law does not bend or alter itself based on opinion or intellectual constructions invented by mankind.

It is fear, indeed fear, the first potential of the animal – conceptualized into all kinds of mental blinds that prevents man from calmly learning about himself and his true nature as an eternal Soul first, and mortal man second.

Yours, Chris

©

Chris Letter 29

The Christian bible is one of the first widely advertised messages to man at large that each one of us has a Soul. A Soul that is common to us all - existing and born from a higher dimension than the physical, lower order of life that we now reside in. However the Soul remains attached and within – the core engine of life that remains inviolate and untouched by the coarse, survival driven surroundings of earth life. Within that Soul is a vast stream of recorded knowledge and intelligence that exceeds all the combined libraries of higher learning on earth. How can this possibly be you say? The answer is simple: You have lost knowledge by assuming the cloak of the physical. The Soul has access to all recorded knowledge in the universe. All events, thoughts, words and deeds are indeed recorded in the data base of life and universal existence, and are available for view by an advanced Soul. However, you will not find the pass code by searching the physical net-works of Earth. You can receive knowledge and wisdom from earthly sources, but it is the Soul that must be unlocked and accessed for progression to be made. You must tap your ancient heritage of life that reaches far beyond your limited earthly circumstances. Therein you will find the answers to the grand dilemma mankind faces with the physical entrapment of his Soul.

Make no mistake, your issues of the day and of life are not with your brother, or God; rather they are with self, for the responsibility of choice in the taking of the original step into the strange land of earth's existence with all its traps and pitfalls to the Soul. God did not tell you or direct you to the earth. Indeed, each took their own first step, and the Karma ensued for each.

In that all must return to earth in their cyclic works of karmic restitution of past earthly misdeeds, the fear doctrine has been carried with you from earth cycle to earth cycle. Indeed, all your experiences, deeds and events are logged and stored by self. Your personality remains intact - even as you go from earth, to Spirit, to earth in succession many times over. All is stored intact in the many levels of mind as to conscious, subconscious and unconscious. Thus, as each earth journey is completed and the physical is left behind, a review of self can be conducted in Spirit. In essence, a counting of deeds is made and one assesses themselves as to their progress made on earth. It is in this conducting of your own spiritual review, that your ultimate purpose rings out most clear – and that is the laying of all Karma to rest as you progress through each lifetime.

If all things experienced in all lifetimes were a part of your conscious awareness, you would short circuit. It would be too much to handle. Thus, the Soul enacts vibrational protection mechanisms in the form of levels of consciousness as you enter each earth journey from one lifetime to another. However, once entry into the coarse fray of earth, awareness and knowledge is lost; and this is a grand part of the dilemma of mankind – to somehow make their way through the Karmic maze of life, wandering the earth in search of our true purpose.

Christ came to earth to inform man that we are all eternal beings, and do not suffer the same death of our biology. We live on in Spirit – always. However, mankind has been taught a certain fear doctrine lifetime after lifetime in a world that never stops its flow onward. This grand hoax has created deeply imbedded attachments to such doctrine that results in a constant swirl of confusion while on earth. It was the Church of Man that excluded and changed the epistles from the man Jesus. All clear references to man's cyclical return to earth for the purpose of Karmic restitution were excluded and removed. Religion was constructed very early on with the purpose of binding mankind to the middle man. Thus the Church would survive. Ah yes, note the reference to survival, which is the base instinct of all physical creatures.

However, mark well and clear little ones of earth, it is not the doctrine or religion of man that allows your body, mind and Soul the wherewithal, and ability to make a choice to pursue or create false doctrine. It is the higher Laws of Soul, in the non physical dimension that allows for, and fuels your very existence in the field of choice. So you see, you are indeed free, unbound, and unfettered, and may proceed without fear of being excluded from life ever lasting. No man is your keeper.

Yours, Chris

©

Chris Letter 30

If the man Jesus, known as the Christ, were to return to you this day upon earth, what would he say unto you?

His words would be of the greatest simplicity, yet of the greatest power – that of a Soul; a perfected Soul. He would say love thy self and love thy neighbor and in this manner may you make gain.

Perhaps man would respond: Oh, but we have tried such simplicities of spirit and look where we have arrived – a world full of pain and sorrow. He would say in return: Is it because you gave in brief attempt to love self and others that your world is falling, and is it because you did not sustain yourself in love to self and others that your world falls? Indeed you must sustain your love, for it is your love in the giving that is infinite and truly sustainable. Your anger and your hate are temporary, though devastating. Your love is infinitely available to give. It matters not the reaction of another. It matters only your own in the giving. Give not with condition. Give not with reservation; give only in the quiet even pulse of your Soul. Ask not for acknowledgment and recognition. Still your mind from the attempt to grasp. You see, one need not advertise their gift of love to another. Such is recorded for all time by your very own Soul.

Fear not that they shall not receive, for the receiving is assured in the giving, despite some outward appearances. Press on little ones; give at all earthly costs, for the earth shall never give payment to your Soul, though your Soul may give to all that is about you. Give onward and steadily in the quiet even pulse of eternal love, and your bounty in return will be fully secured.

Yours, Chris

©

How must we know the way of loving our selves and our neighbor? How is such a thing done with all manner of grace and sensibility? Must we shout our love to the world at large – for all passersby to stop and take certain note? Or should we proceed with great, even calm and simply proffer that measure of good will we are capable of in constant. Indeed, it is the latter. For as you so proceed in good will with full constancy of purpose, so shall you begin to uplift self.

Should we take all monies in hand and all that is excess to ourselves and convey such immediately to those less fortunate? Or should we proceed to do such as we are inwardly able to do? It has been said that it is easier to pass a camel through the eye of a needle than for A rich man to divest his earthly accounts. Why is it that the lump of fear jumps to our throats when we even consider such a divesting of even our excess?

It is because you have forgotten the Law. Indeed, you may proceed to give at your own measure. However, know well and clear that it is the Law which states that the giving of it shall not drain your lamps. Rather the contrary. Your lamps shall overflow with bounty in all that you may need so as you give freely.

Does it matter the amount? Indeed not, for what of the woman in ancient times who gave her last coin and such was her sum total possession. She gave it freely and in turn she was set free – not to abandonment of some cold fate, but to the bounty of return so as the Law states.

You have lost knowledge, therefore you fear to give. It is the fear that halts us. It is the fear that must be released and banished from our hearts. Then as you proceed to give without fear and without condition, so shall the giving return to you with great and wonderful dividends.

Fear not little ones the Law will provide!

Yours, Chris

©

Chris Letter 32

If Christ were to return to this very day in your world, and declare himself openly to the proclaimed keepers of his faith; what would he say to such weighty company of man???

He would assemble all leaders of all faiths, and especially that one perpetrated in his name. Upon assembly he would say unto all of them: "Gather up your riches, your great worldly possessions, all of your monuments and convert them all to gold. Then take the gold and place it into a cauldron of fire and let it all melt itself down until it is cool and fit for dispersal. At that point take the sum total of all your worldly wealth and riches in gold and go out amongst the poor, starving and less fortunate of the day. As you venture forth, leave behind your robes, hats and collars of fine silk and embroidery, for the poor and starving shall know you NOT by your earthly mark of station, but by your measure of giving.

Give it all and return the Church of Man to the Soul of each where it belongs.

Give it all in one day and worry not for the day to come, for if you give it now, and fear not the consequences, then the next day shall come in that same measure of grace and love; and not in the fear in which your are accustomed to".

He would say: "Return the church to thine Souls. Eliminate the middle man, for he is not needed. My church is within each and need go no further beyond in the makings of worldliness". Indeed, this is what he would say to them.

Yours, Chris

©

Indeed, in this world of ours we are taught that if we give of ourselves and then do not immediately receive back - that all is lost. So on we go; as the span of years come to us and then leaves us, we give less and less. For over time, we become part of the harshness of the world. We become less and less as the child we once were, giving freely – until we forget that we were ever once a free spirited giving, child.

Is it the harshness of the world itself that causes us to lose the light of ourselves, or is it because we have removed the candle of love's flame from our own view? Indeed, it is the latter. For as each of you continue to snuff out the light of love, it is not the world that shall suffer your spite, as shall you suffer in the wake of your own self imposed darkness.

Take care to view all in the light of love and compassion, for as you do, no matter what the outward appearances may be, those that cross your path shall recall your love in good time; and as you give and emit your light, your Soul will rejoice within, and that joy of self shall see fit to surface in your consciousness one day; then another, and still another, until that joy becomes a part of your totality of self. Give your light and your love, then, let it be, for it shall return to you – perhaps in your own greatest moment of need.

Yours, Chris

©

Chris Letter 34

He would say to you: Indeed it takes great intellect of mind to argue and justify policy and doctrine. It takes great pride of mind to uphold and practice the doctrine. Then, as well, it takes great recognition of stature to be widely known for your pride and your intellect. Indeed, but what does it take to be known for your love, your kindness, your compassion, and your giving hand. Nothing more than your simple choice to do so; and better for it, as when you love and show kindness, will you have to argue for its policy? And when you show love you shall not have to demonstrate great pride for it; and when you count your worldly deeds you shall not have to puff up like a big balloon so the world may see your great stature. No, you may indeed discard such worldly traits as boastful pride and superior intellect, for they are not necessary in the giving from each and all Souls.

You see, it is an illusion that the world is reserved for those who make good their public display; for what of the rest of all other little ones who are greatest in number and equal in Soul, but of less contrivance. Indeed, what of them? Well, it is so that it is they who are truly blessed that go quietly about extending their hand - loving thy self and thy neighbor in gladness of spirit and heart, for they shall inherit more than the earth. They shall inherit all the power and glory of the kingdom of the Soul re-perfected.

Now, it is also so that those who bluster and make light of a kind word shall also one day come round–about – but only in their own time; and oh what sorrow and sadness it is to their very own Soul that their true purpose so escapes them. Indeed, one may step up the earthly ladder and entertain high worldly regard, but mark well and clear, the Soul has no use for such things and in so doing it is the waiting game you play.

Yours, Chris

©

Chris Letter 35

How many and whoever is it that cries out my name in the stillness of the night?

Do they think that by crying out to me that somehow as a perfected spirit of person – a Soul, that I may somehow personally answer fully to the needs of each as the hue and cry is raised? They think that as a person, a Soul, that I am God to all others. I am not. I am as are all little ones in the great potential of Soul. One who has righted his ship and then returned to you in ancient times to merely show you that it is the eternal Soul that I advertise: The Soul of each one in their own possibilities, not I as a man - a man who would be king or proctor and flit about rendering judgment upon each one of you. Though I am indeed fully aware of the hue and cry rose from your dilemma, and may assist in certain ways, I am not able as a single solitary Soul to expressly fulfill the needs of all. Each Soul in their own inherent quality of infinite being shall attend to their own needs in their own time, for it is your own responsibility to do so. Does this mean that all are alone, and I care not for you, or that Spirit will not assist you? On the contrary, you are surrounded by loving Spirit Souls and Angels from the higher dimension, and my love is so great that it is my vow of Soul to return again and again at the appropriate moment until the un-garbled word has been set before you.

When this time comes, there shall be no raising of dead bodies from earthly graves. There shall be no clap of thunder and a charge of white horses coming forth from the heavens. No indeed, my return shall be marked by a very still calm. And from whence I come you shall not know, and you shall not be met by a parade and great charge; and those who await me in their worldly, self appointed, favored status are in for a very big surprise.

They shall not know me by their minds – only by their Soul shall they know me; and those who do know me shall not be surprised but glad of heart, for such shall mark the start of a new age of peace – not of boastful pride and worldly intellect, but of the Soul's simplicity of love and joy and the extended hand of giving to all class of men. Indeed all.

Yours, Chris

©

Chris Letter 36

Upon my return, I would say to those who seek me out and would listen to my words: Do not fear the changes and aberrations of the earth, for they only reflect the natural, timeless rhythm of the earth and the cosmos.

Is it not odd how they coincide with the disruptive changes in mans social order. Indeed they do, and indeed it is NOT odd. For, the collective Soul of man is attuned where the collective mind is not. Why, what is there to fear by any measure? Is not your Soul and identity of self untouchable by these many impressive events? Indeed it is. You are eternal beings. Entire planetary systems may come and go – while you remain. Your Soul has already witnessed such events and it is not your Soul that cries out in anguish and fear. Indeed it is but the mind of man that has become imbedded with the fear of the survival instinct – that runs like an engine through the span of earth life existence.

No little ones; take great solace and comfort in the fact that you remain intact no matter how dire outer circumstances may be. The most catastrophic and painful a life ending event may be, the Soul finds itself still vibrantly alive. It shakes off the dust of earths disasters, and presses on for all eternity – which of course is never ending. So still your fears little ones, for all is well, no matter all outward appearances.

Yours, Chris

©

Chris Letter 37

As I look about, I see many things in the face of man in these times. In some I see love and understanding, others display fear and consternation. There is a questioning of why God would betray us with such disruptive events. Does he not recognize that our great cities are filled with his children who suffer and die from these great life ending events. What God would allow such wholesale death and destruction amongst his people? Ah, but it is not God that has deserted you. It is mans ego that would attempt to defy or harshly judge the natural rhythm of nature. You see, the Universe is set by laws of rhythm and motion that give no thought to man's presence. There is no harsh judgment from God. Only the timeless flow of life giving energy that feeds all of existence in its orderly progression and march towards balance.

It is man and his outlook that is imbalanced. He takes the natural flow of nature personal if it goes against his will. It is mans ego that points the finger of blame at an angry God. There is no anger in God, only man has anger and judgment. God allows your imbalanced creations because he has bestowed Choice into all Souls. So it is not God who chooses for you. It is man who chooses for himself, and in great numbers. If his collective and individual choices happen to get in the way of nature in its ebb and flow of events, then so be it. But mark well and good little ones; it is not God that has placed you in the path of natures never ending cycle of events. It is man himself that has done so.

Yours, Chris

©

Chris Letter 38

Perhaps you view my last letter to you as harsh and uncompassionate to all my brothers and sisters of earth. Perhaps you even gather in small groups and question my words. Could they be the same as given long before in different times of old? Could I be the same as in times of old? Indeed I am.

Nothing has changed. Man has no less, nor greater tolerance for truth than in times before. Nature's workings are set by Law, as are the workings of man. Indeed, it is God who sets the Laws of all existence and the orderly workings of all things that exist. All of life proceeds in order, not chaos; and so it is with the workings of man. Only man has a Soul that will allow him to render choices that attempt to vilify and defy nature. In these circumstances where you have attempted to stray far from the principles of the Soul for many thousands of years, it is your Soul along with all the Angels in heaven that stand at the ready in welcome to your return in any given moment. The gates stand ever open, but YOU must choose to enter.

There is an outpouring of love and grace in a constant flow that man does not see with his mind. But his Spirit is attuned to the pulse of this life giving force that is never ending; and it is the Soul that will emerge into your mind in a flood of brilliance and remembrance. For indeed, there is a recorded remembrance of ones true self that is registered deep within each of us. Look to it within and you shall find it; and when that moment comes, you shall know the truth.

Yours, Chris

©

Chris Letter 39

So many of you cry out my name in your most dire moments of need. Should I rush to the assistance of all who would beseech me? No need my little ones as there is indeed already help surrounding you in each and every moment! It is only the dense vibration of earth's existence that hides your view of the next life and its infinite potentials. So you fear greatly the end of your existence here on earth. You clutch to it as a mother clutches her new born to her bosom. Indeed you should value each day of your life here on earth; and use all your faculties to make gain in your heart and Soul, for such will serve you well upon your continuation into the next life.

Do not fear the loss of your physical, as you will look upon it as an encumbrance to your spirit once you have made good your crossing over. There are many now, who cross over in groups. Are they to be lost to wander with their Souls scattered to a new chaotic dimension? Indeed not, each has their place in the realm of spirit. There is life and learning that goes on. Once you are greeted into spirit life, you will find that there is experience, events, laughter and love – much as there was here on earth – only the range of experience and the feeling of it are so much more sharply defined.

You will find yourself surrounded by a vibrant life's experience with great opportunity to learn and progress along your path to re-perfection. Yet all must return to earth at some point to resolve past Karmic debt and also to fulfill your vows of Soul in return with others of like mission. You see little ones life is a rhythmic dance of march and progression through earth and spirit life in fulfilling your quest of return to pure Soul state. Indeed, the earth offers its own experience and in its own way, but do not fear the loss of it, as it is not your heritage, nor is it your true self in expression.

Earth is a sub system of the higher universe and is a part of creation that was better left to itself by all Souls. Now we must make good our journey back to the homeland of pure spirit. Do not fear your existence in the next world, as it contains happier times and great, expansive moments of love and colorful experience not possible on earth.

Indeed, you may call out my name and your own Soul will hear you, as will the Angels in heaven along with others of spirit and good will; and as you pass, you will be met, much as being met by loved ones after a long earth journey. You will disembark from the old life much as a shedding of old ragged clothes, and then re-embark into your new life of the joy laughter and love that awaits you.

Many will grasp and hold fast to the earth - some, not knowing that the passing event has taken place. You must still your fears and release the old life, for that is where death lies – in the past! Look to the beings of light; trust them, as they will escort you out from the old and into the new along a pathway of grace and love. You may hear and see the grieving of loved ones left behind, but you must bless and release them, knowing that the sorrow for them will pass, as it does for all. Time heals all Souls, for all Souls make good their journey home. Does it matter how long the journey made good? Indeed not, for in eternity there really is no time - such is indeed the definition of eternity! There are no dead-lines in spirit, because you – the true you – lives on forever. So, know that your loved ones left behind will shed their loss of you, AND their grief with the passing of life's events. Simply bless them, send your love, then turn to the beings of light and move on. This you must do at a given point – and better sooner than later, for there is no profit to the Soul in remaining. So ease your minds and still your fears little ones, as there is no death – only a renewed life with vast opportunities and experiences So, forgive, and let go of your fears and regrets from the past, and move on.

Yours, Chris

©

Chris Letter 40

All well and good for the next life you might say. But, what of the here and now? What is my purpose? Why am I here? Your purpose is to make good your return to pure spirit - your original form, which is that of Soul with no physical body attached. I say to you that this is a simply defined mission but one little understood by man. The hum of daily events in the act of survival is most effective at covering up your true purpose. The events of the day have no inherent purpose, but only to serve as a vehicle and proving ground for mans true purpose – and that is to take each moment and event and consider, and frame it in the light of love, compassion and forgiveness. Each day is full of opportunities for personal advancement; and mark well; each bit of karma laid to rest shall loom of large benefit to you in the coming age.

There is a shake out – a processing out of earths existence by large groups of Souls who shall be limited in their opportunity to return. Make good each day your advancement, little ones, as the rewards are great as are the penalties. You see, the earth life is most necessary in the process of advancement. For it is in the earth life that you have fallen. Here on earth is where your dues are paid life by life, and bit by bit; and if the opportunity for return begins to close, then ages can pass before the opportunity for resolution may again avail itself to so many of heaven and earth. Do I speak in riddles to you? Indeed I do not. I merely would implore my fellow Souls to awaken quickly to your own true purpose, and work each day in a diligent manner to release all past hurts, emotional debts, and any righteous indignation that you may have been clinging to. They are not worth the price of ones Soul. It is your very own Soul that you must crown as the king of glory. Listen quietly and carefully to its soft urgings and guidance.

It is not the grinding noise of the mind, but the soft gentle urgings from within that will serve you well in all matters. Yes, in all matters, for the Soul can see ahead and make considerations of value and benefit where the mind and the ego cannot go. Listen close and heed well ALL men of earth – yes all men, including those of high station in the order of mans world. Take pause and go deep within self in your private moments and come forth from that place a changed person, for it is time to heed the bell of warning as it rings out to you from these pages. This is your opportunity, and yours to make gain.

Yours, Chris

©

Chris Letter 41

Am I to come forth in a physical body and lead each one of you out of the wilderness? Indeed not. The saving of Souls is not done by another – even from one of re-perfection with the power of life in his hands. Do not look outward and do not stand in waiting. Make all haste to go forth inward. Prepare for the journey inward and launch into the deep. Dare to be kind and forgiving. Dare to release old scores and hatreds. For when you settle accounts with another, you are really settling your own accounts. The great secret of life and healing is that I am not needed for such. I did not come to be king of life, or even king of heaven or earth. I came for one single, simple purpose; and that was to deliver the good news of eternal life of the Souls of all, and that each possesses the wherewithal within self to practice the Soul principles – and thus bit by bit, make their own way homeward. You see little ones, Christ consciousness need only be tapped by self. No one man is the inventor of such, nor is he gate keeper. The gates are always open to those who would make the inner gain and pass through. The Law of Christ Consciousness will not allow you to ascend until you yourself decide to release your Karma and embrace love and forgiveness. There is no guard detail that stands at the gates of heaven. The gates remain open for all eternity and shall never close to you.

I tell you boldly and squarely that it is all up to you and you alone. I cannot lay hands upon you and clear your Karma, for; it is yours in the making and yours in the undoing. So do not become as a maid in waiting – go forth into the uncharted lands of the Soul ways while here on earth. Do not wait for your passing to take up spirit's way. For, if you wait, you may suffer great anguish at all the lost opportunities - and even greater anguish if there is no admittance into the new age. The new age is coming. Mark well as the signs are already upon you. There will be a paring, and those left will be of higher consciousness, but not necessarily of higher worldly station. So you must peer within and count your words and deeds – and if the scales tip away from love, kindness and forgiveness, then make great haste to reverse your direction. The earth is entering a new cycle and mankind will follow suit. Consider wisely your inner position. Proceed into your quietest place and sum up your life. Take honest stock with yourself. Make your change for the better, then, go forth into the world a changed person – that always has a smile and kindness readily at hand.

I say to you now. Does it take a great leader of men to assist you in this, or perhaps inspire you to action? Indeed not. It is only your own simple choice to do so; and well advised you are to awaken to your Soul within. Trust; yes trust that your very own Soul will guide you from out of the wilderness. You must only decide to go within and listen to the calm gentle urgings. They are always there – round the clock, as the Soul and spirit never sleep. It is of another dimension where sleep is not required for sustenance. So, no need to wait for some special day or hour. Make your bid now little ones, for now is all that you will ever have.

Yours, Chris

©

Chris Letter 42

Indeed little ones, I am with you all in spirit, for it is my vow to attend to all of earth until the very last Soul has made good their journey in return. I cannot do it for you, but it is my Soul commitment to assist you in any and all ways. This assistance comes in many forms: From both spirit and from the physical life setting as well. These letters written to you are a perfect example of my commitment. The purveyor of these letters to you has made a similar vow long ago to carry forth my message to you. Know full and well that there are many Souls of spirit and of earth's journey who are fully engaged in the assistance to man. The credo is: Not one Soul lost. For, no matter how lost a Soul may be in regression, there is only one final outcome – and that is a full and complete return to the father. Indeed – to a full state of grace that radiates love and beauty throughout all of heaven and earth. Difficult to imagine for some – ah yes indeed it is; but I say to you with no equivocation whatsoever: Not one Soul lost. You see, it is only your power of choice that gives you the way to fall from grace. But, it is your fundamental nature to return to a state of grace. You can go against your nature, but you cannot escape your nature, therefore, you shall return – in time. Am I concerned with your time to make restitution? Ultimately no, for there is no time in eternity. You are eternal because you ARE your Soul, and it is your SOUL that is eternal. So, no, I do not grow weary of your seemingly endless plight. I shall stay the course, for as one who can see ahead to the final glorious outcome, I am well fortified.

I have the power of life and the knowledge of life in its totality of existence. I can see and witness the dance of the Universe as it pulses and vibrates in perfect balance and harmony; and so shall each one of you see this – all in your own time. There is no judgment of you from here; only understanding of your plight. It is no sacrifice for me to attend to your plight and it is no sacrifice for me to return to you one day again to apply my full being in the never ending quest for the full return of all little ones to grace. Is it fraught with risk? Indeed it is. The risk is in the return and exposure to all of the pitfalls of earths pull to temptation. Ah yes, it is the same for me as it is for all of you. I am a Soul with the power of choice to fall just as you are; and that is why we are all of a common purpose and brotherhood. You see, we are inextricably all connected and bonded together. None are separate. We are all part of, and connected to the one Soul, and therefore cannot escape the bond of one another.

Now I know that man is divided into different camps on earth and that one is pitted against the other; but one day this will end, and you shall see these divisions of man against himself crumble into the dust of the ages. How do I know this? It is because I see and know the nature of man and his outcome both in past, present and in the coming ages. It is a view that is available to one of grace, and know full and well that each one of you, in your own time, shall be of the same state of grace. I speak to you almost conversationally in this fashion, as I wish you to have a sense of our common bond in our brotherhood. I am not over you as some would be – master proctor – no; I am just a Soul, a little one who has made the journey home.

Now, I say to you with all the power and humility of my re-perfected state: Cast off all of the ragged clothing that you can, here and now. Break down the doors to your Soul and engage your true self fully. You will not find sacrifice and deprivation in the house of your Soul. Only joy, laughter and love that you have not known for a time – but shall be familiar to you once revisited. It is no loss to you, only huge gain for you to engage your true self. Make haste, for while the Soul is eternal in its quest, the earth processes through its own natural cycles without regard to the presence of man. The earth is your proving ground in the Karmic dance of all mankind; and because of its cyclic nature, there can be disruption and your quest can be delayed. Therefore, I urge one and all to take great heed from my message of love to you. Embrace your true self within. Reverse your direction and make gain. I can promise you that the rewards are without limit, and that one day you shall know them with unfathomable joy and gratitude.

The time has now come for me to sign off, but my presence is no less. I am truly with each one of you in the bond of Soul and Spirit. I shall never abandon you – ever. I am here – as I always have been here for you, for you see, we are all one. So, it can be no other way. In these many pages you have been given all that you need to proceed out of the darkness – to no longer be lost and in wonderment of purpose.

Heed well these words of wisdom, as they are drawn from the book of life that God has laid down for us all. As I depart these pages, know that I am not far – my Spirit never leaves you, as you never leave mine. Know that we shall meet again – both in heaven and on earth.

Yours, Chris

©

Printed in the United States
By Bookmasters